A Garden Full of Weeds

Jean McArthur

A Garden Full of Weeds

Acknowledgements

Some of the poems in *A Garden Full of Weeds* have been previously published in *Cut on the Bias – a collection of poems and sketches by Jean McArthur*, 1994, Panopticon Publishing House, and in *Vintage series – Stories, Poetry, Prose from Penola Festivals*, 1996–2002, edited by Marg Muller.

A Garden Full of Weeds was funded by a Federal government mentorship grant through Country Arts SA.

Thanks go to Jude Aquilina for her suggestions, encouragement and consistent support over a three-year period. Aside from being a mentor, she has also become a friend.

I wish to thank the following for their support in the publication of this volume: Bev Puckridge, Merilyn de Nys and Lucia Pichler.

Gratitude also to Stephen Matthews, who accepted my work for publication, and to Byron Robbie for having enough faith in me to purchase a copy in advance!

A Garden Full of Weeds
ISBN 978 1 74027 797 6
Copyright © Jean McArthur 2013

First published in this form 2013
Reprinted 2015

GINNINDERRA PRESS
PO Box 3461 Port Adelaide SA 5015
www.ginninderrapress.com.au

Contents

Foreword	9
Limestone Coast, SA	11
Kintyre	13
Cape Martin	14
Gravenstein Apples	15
Nora Creina, 1950s	16
Nan	17
Furner School	18
To Mount Burr	20
A Ticket to the Sun	21
1 Sun – Lizard	23
2 Sun – Melanoma	24
Emergency	25
Lesley	26
Hernia to Death	27
Swallows	28
Avalanche	29
Headache	31
A Dry State in a Dry Land	33
Wild Wind	35
Radiata	36
Snuggery Pulp Mill	37
Naked	38
Bridal Creeper	39
Seacliff Garden	40
Desert Camp Ground	41
Oodnadatta	42
Summer Rain	43
The East Wind	45
Sydney	47
Five-pound Start	49
Baklava	51

Anzac	52
Milford Sound	53
Cedar and Snow	55
Western Red Cedar	57
Shipboard	58
Cariboo Range	59
Lac Des Roches	60
Futility	61
Washing Day	62
Wood Grain	64
Chilcotin Fall	65
Testing	66
Mink	67
Loon	69
A Restless Wind	71
Basilica	73
Fiftieth Summer	74
Lime Marmalade	75
Bill	76
Lawn Bowls	77
Discipline	78
Hey Diddle Diddle	79
Morning Death	80
Achievements	81
From Mariachi to Jazz	83
Mexican	85
Teotihuacán	86
Olmec Heads*	87
Mexico	88
Hammock	89
Zócalo	90
New Orleans	92
Breast Cancer	93
1995	95

Premonition	96
Destiny	97
Breast Cancer	98
May '95, Thinking…	99
Fog	100
Nasturtiums	101
Green Tea and Rice	103
Siam Morning	105
Curd and Treakle	106
Mangoes 1	107
Mangoes 2	108
Nirvana	109
Mandalay Music	110
Kites	111
Malaysian Pewter	112
Charcoal and Ashes	113
Fire	115
With Apologies to Friedrich Nietzsche	116
To 19 Jardine Street	117
Adrift	119
Threads	120
Paper Phantoms	121
Homesick	122
Numb	123
Forty	124
Changing Weather	125
Magpies	127
Red Flags	128
Confetti	129
Seasons	130
Balancing Lovers	132
Monsoon	133
Toothmarks	134
Amber	135

For my mother, Hilda, who taught me to see

and my father, Jack, who taught me to sing

Foreword

Jean McArthur grew up on a sheep farm among the old limestone coastlines of southern South Australia. On a windswept plain, 'Kintyre' began as two rooms built of limestone and a wooden horse-drawn cabin. It developed in stages and eventually became surrounded by casuarinas – tough nuggetty trees with long needles which sigh in the wind.

Jean travelled firstly in books, and then wandered around Australia for ten years, working mostly as a registered nurse in operating theatres. A foreign friend lured her to explore the world, in fits and starts. Always gathering addresses, a few sketches, notes, friends, materials, tokens and papers, Jean would leave them packed in boxes and bags at her parents' home.

When she finally came back to Australia, she bought a post-war austerity cottage in Mt Gambier in the Limestone Coast district. With three chooks to share a garden full of weeds, she returned (for the fifth time) to work as a registered nurse in the operating theatres at the local hospital. On her annual leave she camped in various parts of Australia or explored countries closer to this continent.

In 1990 she and husband Jim had an extended backpacking visit to Mexico and Central America, following La Ruta de Maya. In 2000, they backpacked around northern South America and were in Brazil when the cottage at Jardine Street, Mt Gambier, burnt down.

Jean is now rebuilding – garden, home, lifestyle – escaping intermittently to visit friends. Her drawings and works on paper are exhibited regularly with Thumbprint and in Gallery 54, Penola. Jean now lives in a beautiful modern home full of triangles and blue for serenity. She continues to write verse about the weather, places she has been and people she has known. In quiet moments, words march through her head rhythmically, probably an echo from childhood, when her parents read and recited poetry before bedtime.

Limestone Coast, SA

Kintyre

They speak of prairie flatness
yet I've never seen
a land as flat as that where I was born.
We could see as far as far
until the earth curved
in all directions bar the east,
where distant scrub
muffled the horizon.

Other views punctuated
only by stark white gums –
killed by lightning or grubs long before.
Nothing to stop southern blasts
across oceans from Antarctica.

Our home, cocooned in casuarinas
shielded us from bleak
chilblain dampness.
Braced against wet westerlies,
it faced east towards the sun.

Cape Martin

Salty bushes
clinging
to rain-battered sand
no horizon
sky blurring into
the grey-green
coldly angry sea
that grumbles, rolling
retreating and rolling again
lashing at the shore
tossing torn seaweed
pink and green and brown
in tangled masses
shiny, slippery
cords and pods
tan, umber, sepia
tapestry on grained gold
woven, braided, divided, twisted
magenta, lime and pink.
Sea swirls, sweeping
seething, hissing
flinging onto rocks
fragmenting into foam.

Gravenstein Apples

The first clean taste of Gravenstein
fills my head with childhood images

long hot days in summer
        sprinklers on the grass,
cold mutton, tomatoes,
        persistent blowfly buzz,
acrid sheep dip smell,
        the feel of steady heat,
                superphosphate's sting.

I run beneath a rotating sprinkler,
        gasping as cold bore water
washes away sights,
        smells and sounds,
leaving only
        the clean, fresh taste
                of Gravenstein.

Nora Creina, 1950s

Nora Creina – a childhood paradise,
the name rolls off my tongue.
She was a ship that sank and gave
the sheltered bay her name.
A wild island, only low-tide access
shielded harbour waters, cool and green.

Deep in boobialla scrub was a huge clan tent
where Fergusons would eat and talk:
cousins, aunts and uncles came and went at will.
Miles of beach, acres of scrub, cliffs to climb
and our 'house' in wave-carved rocks,
to hide inside or meet imaginary friends.

Morning crays were boiled in a kerosene tin
on a stone fireplace then hung by their tails to dry.
The men fished daily from Stinky Bay,
we'd all go down to the beach to meet
the chugging boat with its load of sweep
or other fish of the day.

We'd splash in the waves when it was hot,
but on greyer days we played Cooncan
or explored sandhills, picking muntries
by the billy-full.   A tent of our own
to sleep in, the lull of ocean's roar and the wind
from boobiallas caressing our canvas walls.

Nan

Drysdale, Millicent North, SA, 1940s

Staying at my grandmother's home,
sounds come floating through the years
bringing a spread of pictures:
crackling fire in the old wood stove
big black kettle singing;
sunshine through afternoon windows
and pomegranate leaves;
ticking clock on the mantelpiece
pendulum's relentless swinging.

Laugh of kookaburra echoes
from stringy-barks where low,
bendy branches were our swings.
Carrying a few sticks of wood
through the propped open door,
comes my Nan singing 'Galway Bay'.
I see her yet when I hear that song.

She crosses the creek in winter's flow
on a row of stepping stones –
white against black mud.
Bent back, laughing eyes,
Nan finds goodies in her pantry –
a few sultanas, an apricot.
I feel her warmth now as I sit
at this scrubbed wooden table
staying at my grandmother's home.

Furner School

I remember Furner School – tall, wooden walls,
a single room with porch attached,
huge pine trees, golden springtime wattle.

I remember Moles's chooks, three feet tall at least,
they'd snatch your lunch right from your hand
if you stood too near their fence.

And I know Paddy Melon Corner, where Cobb and Co.
went on to Gillap. We turned left
to rescue tadpoles in ever-evaporating puddles.

I can see ten thousand rabbits – a moving sea
between fern covered sandy banks
and damp flats where fresh grass grew.

I remember the old school bend,
tank stand rubble, pepper trees,
dangling berries, spicy red.

Down the yard, school garden plots:
mine was triangular with a daisy bush,
and william, sweet sweet william.

I can see winter water overflowing
at Ey's bend – wading through,
and musky, muddy tortoises.

I remember Clifford's shop at one end of Kintore Inn,
liquorice chews, fizzy sherbets in a paper bag;
bright lollies tempting we who had no coins.

The opposite end was Teacher's home, with
tartan rugs and lanterns, ice chest inside asbestos walls.
Their veranda was a stage for Christmas plays.

The next teacher refused to live in such dereliction.
I don't recall rotting floors, cracked walls, or salt damp.
I sensed only warmth, happiness

                        and my first-ever friend.

To Mount Burr

Yellow ochre paddocks
        race away
to dusky blue,
        undulating
along the edge
        of moody sky,
grey and white
        in stripes,
                and bands,
                      and layers,
like a Guatemalan scarf.

A Ticket to the Sun

1 Sun – Lizard

Being born in summer
to February's heat
I feel the need of sun
upon my skin,
like a desert lizard
with intricate brocade,
scale-like tribal design.

When he, with venom,
called me lizard
accused me
of not emerging
from my rock until
the Fahrenheit was eighty,
I smiled for all my harmless kin,
I longed to yawn,
show him my blue tongue
then turn to wander
over red wind-patterned sand,
slowly,
leaving only footprints
and waving tail line.

2 Sun – Melanoma

Being born in summer
to February's heat,
I feel the need
of sun on my skin.
I know of melanomas:
dark marks on dermis
from the rays of sun,
I know the hurt to all –
slowly sapping, eating,
from inside out.
The pain, the black,
until the victim goes,
willingly, into the dust
of this ochre land.
Yet still I feel
the need of sun
on my skin.

Emergency

Mildura, Victoria

The first emergency surgery
        I ever saw
was a tangled mass
        of bone and bowel and blood.
Not even the surgeon
        knew where to start.
'You stand there,' Sister said
        putting me against a wall.
They patched him up
        as best they could,
sat him in an oxygen tent
        for three days till he died.
He was driving his son to hospital –
        'Appendicitis' they said,
from somewhere 'out the Millewa'
        a hundred miles or so.
Hit a post on a long straight road –
        impaled by his steering wheel.
The small boy was not hurt at all
        went home next day,
complete with his appendix –
        but no father.

Lesley

Today is your birthday,
and so
I thought of you.
Remember
when we used to go
down by the river bank
or drive north
along dusty red?

The world was open
to us then.
A string of places
come to mind:
Werrimull, Deniliquin,
Old Euston Station,
Campbelltown and
lastly Ipswich
and that big Queenslander.

I see mostly heat, dust,
dirty feet and shorts.
Through my thoughts
the river runs
tirelessly, timelessly
whirling sad times
to deep pools
or rippling laughter
through Lock Ten.

Hernia to Death

Dallas, Texas

Glad when I heard he died
sad for his friends and kin.
Although I hardly knew the man
his name and his anatomy
were familiar to me.
He came to hospital to have
his hernia repaired.
A simple operation –
he'd be out within a week.
Inactivity showed
his circulation wasn't good.
We cleared an artery in his left leg –
still it clogged so back he came
for a bypass with a graft.
That didn't work, so late one night
we chopped his leg in half.
His right vein then blocked too –
I cried when I saw his name
for a second amputation.
Six months and nine surgeries
from the time he came to us
he died in his sixty-fourth year.

Swallows

Outside work's window
rigid geometric concrete
straight lines, squares, rectangles
orderly and regimented.

In contrast, an anxious northerly
cuffs the ears of distant trees.
Then within my glass rectangle,
a flight of swallows – hundreds maybe –
coming from nowhere, wheeling, circling,
each in its own orbit.

They rest briefly on the gutter
pleating wings, then, away, whirling,
mesmerising as a dervish, they vanish,
leaving only grey geometry.

Avalanche

Terrace, BC, Canada

I once met a man who was trapped in snow
eight hours in an avalanche.
Daily he drove one hundred miles
delivering the papers and mail.

Snow-covered mountains rose
steep to the north
with tunnels and timber and screes.
In inches between rail, river and road
skunk cabbage bloomed yellow in spring.
The Skeena flowed swiftly with eddies and whirls
to mingle with salt at Prince Rupert.
Lonely bald eagles perched on snags
or soared above, looking for fish.

Only one building between two towns
in a niche on a bend in the river.
Five people had stopped
for news, coffee and pie.
Spring mudslides are common
on those sheer slopes,
rain loosens soil and snow.
Was there a rumble? A warning?
No time for escape.
It buried the roadside café.

Only regulars travelled this road
when black ice was melting and freezing.
A telephone crew arriving for lunch
radioed back for assistance,
they dug out a puppy at first –
then eight bodies –
only one man left alive –
trapped with a pocket of air.

They brought him to the hospital
long hours after his saving,
I heard his voice screaming,
I saw his arms flailing –
his rescuers struck by the blows.
He took a month off,
went back to the road
to his stoic livelihood.

What does he think as he passes each day
that space where the cafe had been?
Does he notice each year by the roadside
skunk cabbage blooming yellow in spring?

Headache

It comes creeping softly
like a sea mist rolling in
engulfing enthusiasm,
cloaking creativity,
burgeoning small tasks,
blurring logic, reason.

Sometimes
it gathers in the night
boring, grinding,
eye piercing pain
pounding into wakefulness.

An ice pack, tablet and prayer
for sleep, blissful sleep.
Even death who always was
a foreigner to me,
seems more friendly now.

A Dry State in a Dry Land

Wild Wind

Limestone Coast, SA

Clouds tumble over one another
bushes hunch to let the wind pass overhead
wild oats jostle on the roadside
stoic clumps of rush stand stiff – resolute
while reeds are twisting and plaiting
and a windmill pumps crazily into the overflow.
Trees bow and bend, trunks braced
twig fingers fidgeting, knuckles clicking.
Are they paying homage
to their own strength,
by defiantly clinging to Mother Earth?

Radiata

South Australia

Armies march to clothe
and conquer scrub
uniform and tall they stand
only to fall themselves
conscripted, devoured
into chips, to be bleached,
brewed and leached,
rolled to tissue
for man to wipe
his anus
and his nose.
Raised and nurtured for
Supreme Sacrifice.

Snuggery Pulp Mill

Westward-flowing flags
flap from chimney stacks
above a glittering city,
dazzling as any Vegas Casino
or Lachlan on the River.
Mountains of chips,
laundered money from Monterey* –
luring students with high stakes
into push-button jobs,
gambling their marriages
with alcohol, boredom, kids –
converting them to ex-husbands,
mere tokens – fat old men
with no homes,
dream horizons fading.

*Pinus Radiata is also known as Monterey Pine.

Naked

Mt Benson, SA

Only bushes curved by wind
mark the eyebrow edge.
Cape Jaffa grapevines flow from scalp,
as tresses over shoulders
spread and drape,
conceal the nape.

Bare-breasted hills,
dip to umbilical undulations.
A patch of bracken grows
between long thighs.
Languorous legs stretch lazily
and loll beneath the sun.

Bridal Creeper

Coorong, SA

Lush green
fine leaves
creeping
crawling
smothering
soft Australian
sage-green foliage

leaving
stark sticks
strangled
bare birch brooms
futile bony fingers
clutching
for the sky.

Seacliff Garden

Yorke Peninsula

Nestled
        among the rocks –
pink petals
        on matted leaves,
fan flowers
        massed blue,
leathery leaves
        repelling
                saline-laden winds.
A tiny wattle
        espaliered
                to the ground,
pink pigface tendrils
        clinging,
                a flattened scaevola bonsai.
Nature blossoming
                on this windswept cliff,
would that my garden
        was exquisitely neat like this
                without wild winds to blow.

Desert Camp Ground

Northern South Australia

At last! Hot showers.
        What a treat.
I need a wash.
But now,
        standing in this
                draughty shower block,
I'm not at all sure
        that I do.
I've not bathed for a week –
        five days or is it six?
Of course I've washed in parts,
        and changed my underwear.
I've become accustomed
        to these clothes,
so snug and cosy.
Do I have to strip?
        To get all wet?
It seems so unappealing.
The water may not
        be hot at all
like the solar ones
        ten days ago.
I have
        a better understanding now
of little boys, or cats
        and old grey men
                in flannel underwear.

Oodnadatta

Have you ever been
to Oodnadatta, where railway lines
go on into infinity
both north, and south,
but no trains ever come?

When the Ghan* came
the town was famous
for its hill of bottles,
the glass molten
by constant sun.

I saw far horizons,
heard a lonely wind
whine slowly across the plain.
I saw a tribal family
in a circle on the ground.

I heard an eerie flapping –
a loose sheet
of corrugated iron,
in a long forgotten fence –
a hollow, empty sound.

Have you ever been
to Oodnadatta, where railway lines
go on into infinity
both north, and south,
but no trains ever come?

*The Ghan is a train which goes twice weekly from Adelaide to Darwin, named after the Afghan cameleers who plied their trade along this route in the late nineteenth century. The line now follows a different route.

Summer Rain

A hot and steamy day
        followed by a thunderstorm,
with rain
        falling by the inch.
All the trees and earth
        drinking their fill.
It washed and cleansed
        the leaves, the roofs, the paths.
Sounds of wetness all around:
        water dripping, crickets singing,
gutters running, splashing,
        drumming on the roof,
leaving our world
        cool and misty for a day.
Plants seem to swell
        drooping heavily,
as if to brace themselves
        for tomorrow's heat.

The East Wind

Sydney

New South Wales

I have loved you, Sydney, your many faces –
   some now forever gone.
I have trodden your busy streets,
   walked your flowing footpaths
      in equinoctial rain.

I've climbed summer steps of Tamarama Bay,
   seen Bondi bodies
      filled with Sunday sand.
I've crammed Friday's lunchtime minutes
   with Paddy's Market smells and sounds
      a myriad for the senses, intermingling.

I have stayed in colonial grandeur
   been poor in Railway Square
      with cigarette and black coffee lunch.
I have seen you naked Anzac morning
   with Rosemary, piquant Rosemary
      for remembrance.

I have run through your back allies
   when my bus was late,
savoured hamburgers at The Quay –
   lured by onion frying in shopfronts
      tempting me to spend my bus fare home.

I have sat guiltily staring out night window
   ignoring 'Fares, please' from conductor,
have pitied Paddington's slums
   with Hill's hoist sized backyards –
      now upmarket town houses.

I've stared into your harbour waters
   from the Mosman ferry bow,
       smelt frangipani on the breeze,
as the ferry, rocking gently,
   soothed workday cares away
       and eased Friday's frazzled nerves.

Five-pound Start

Brisbane, 1962

I arrived with five borrowed pounds.
The first went to the People's Palace*
plus five shillings key deposit
for a room where one could not turn
between wardrobe and bed –
sausages for breakfast, though.

Bought a coffee, map and paper
over which to pore to find a roof.
Bus ticket to the cheapest place –
but slunk away unnoticed, from grime
and dilapidation – discouraged,
I then walked to all the rest.

In Teneriffe, high above the Valley,†
a girls' hostel backed onto a ravine,
a swimming pool overlooked by café seats,
cupboards full of crockery, three gas stoves.
Downstairs, penny-slotted washing coppers,
for twenty-seven and six a week.

On a nearby vacant lot, the local market
with board and trestle tables held
pawpaws for a shilling each;
sixpence for a huge brown bag of beans;
coffee; rice and sugar. Thirty shillings left.
Only coins after next week's rent.

I scan papers for employment,
applications, interviews –
'Sorry, nothing doing.'
Green beans and rice, hot and filling –
pawpaw breakfast, quite exotic –
gave stamina to walk Valley streets
asking for a job.

An emerging artist humbly
gives thirty shillings for an hour's pose –
enough to pay late rent for two more weeks.
Then a steady job
of placing bottles on a belt
and packing Panda chips
at last allows bus fares,

        evening dances and to repay my debt.

---

* People's Palace: Salvation Army establishment for cheap food and accommodation after World War II.

† Valley: Fortitude Valley, a central Brisbane suburb, now a nightlife hub, but not in 1962.

Baklava

Sydney, 1963

Pitt Street, Sunday,
walking home from work –
no food, no money.
Behind Greek glass,
locked and barred,
wispy, tempting:
honey sweet baklava.
Dripping diamond shapes.
My empty eyes devouring,
hollow stomach longing.
I light my last cigarette
and wander on.

Anzac

Sydney, 1963

April morning
grey skies weep.
Six o'clock street
bare and peaceful
my footsteps echo.
A solitary crumpled newspaper
skitters erratically
over the pavement.

Martin Place
waits tidily for the parade.
First arrival –
a truckload of rosemary.
Aroma of grey days, old friends
dead kin, war and peace
faded photographs and youth
blood, mud and laughter,
slanting autumn sunshine.
'Taps'* echoes in the hollow street.

* Taps: officially 'Butterfield's Lullaby', also known as 'Day is Done', played on a bugle or trumpet for evening lights-out at military ceremonies and funerals.

Milford Sound

Thin rain misting, drifting,
the day we went to Milford
passed Lake Te Anau Au,
cold green waters rippling, tossing,
then on into mist lost mountains.
An eeriness closed in on us
as we stopped at Homer's Tunnel –
one way only each half hour.

Did we get it right?
How horrible to meet halfway
someone from the Other Side.
Out at last to ethereal dampness
land of fiords, and sea fogs;
down navy mountain slopes
waterfalls mingled with rain,
stringing, spangling silver threads.

The Milford Store's reality
adjusted my psyche with
hot food and people –
we floated on a small white launch
into clinging fog.
Ghostly seabirds glided silently
in and out of view.

Our laughter and chatter
absorbed by spongy air.
Thin dampness seeped into bones.
We did not see the Tasman Sea
at the fiord's end.
We did not see Mitre Peak
except in postcards, but at least
we sensed the essence of that
deep unearthly fiord land.
Thin rain misting, drifting,
hiding secrets, myths and Maori legends.

Cedar and Snow

Western Red Cedar

Stately shape, graceful branches,
drooping, interlocking segments.
I love its spicy aroma
the feel of its linear grain.
Others like it too:
for kindling because
it splits so well,
for bean poles or tomato stakes;
shakes and shingles
moss covered on cabins
that meld, blending with the forest.
I have smelt it lining bathrooms
of the well-to-do,
seen it burned and shaped and turned
into all imaginable things,
carved grave markers or totems tall.
Poles carry power through rain and snow
for Pacific North West's light.
I've seen its broken limbs and fingers
in the clear-fell on the ground.
I don't want it to line my bathroom –
although in truth I do
I want it to be wild and free
on steep Canadian slopes,
giving life to totems
Raven, Bear and Thunderbird.

Shipboard

I first saw him among people on the stairs,
his gaunt, cropped hair a sombre stroke
against a vibrant holiday world.
He could have been a criminal
just released from jail, a rogue,
intent on working through the ship –
he surely needed laughter.
That night I heard him
speaking German to someone I knew,
so set out to make him smile.
It was my determination,
drawn masochistically to impale
myself on spinous words
eat his poisonous conversation.

Seven years he took to win.
It was I who cried
as words shifted, twisted,
just enough to alter meaning.
Swept by the tide of travel,
my swimming arms weakened
so much so I almost drowned.
He saw, pushed me to the shore.
Was pity, power or freedom his motivation?
I crawled along the beach
naked, stripped of camouflage
until my legs grew strong enough
to climb dunes or cliffs
and be gone.

Cariboo Range

BC, Canada

Have you ever been
to the top of the world
above timberline where
the sun's rays touch first and last?

Land of long winters,
brief, exalting summers.
Spring slopes and meadows flush with colour
even before the snow is gone,
Flower fields of Hiawatha's heaven,
micro-plants in a tiny world at foot,
above, endless peaks of blue on blue.

Fall brings berries bright and scarlet;
tow-haired, fluffy anemone heads;
matted leaves in autumn hues.

Have you ever slept among the stars
breakfasted with the sun
amid a wild garden
ending only as the world's edge rolls away?

Lac Des Roches

BC, Canada

Full moon, half a moon,
wagon wheels snow etching
muffled white, perspective fluctuating
snow blurred forest, dark shapes emerge
ungainly, throat tassels dangling, tangling
mother moose with echoing calf
scrambling across slick road.

Timber cabin, warm brown wood
elk antlers nailed above the door
icicles from roof edge hanging,
footpath murky, melted mud;
door creaks, bell jangling, boot rack dripping,
coffee aroma merging
with odour of wet mittens.

Residents kill time,
assess strangers, offer greetings, then resume
stories told a hundred times.
Fur-lined jackets, gnarled brown hands
characters from book pages,
cowboy hats, leather boots hand-tooled.
Fly-speckled photographs of local heroes
drawing-pinned to timber walls
small deer antlers fixed in a row above the bar.

Steaming fresh-baked pies,
cherry, apple or blueberries picked last fall
from the meadow by the lake.
Fortified for darkening home trip
white eyes strain for looming moose.

Futility

You were the best lover I knew,
you taught me softly, gently,
but scorned my head
my brain, my thoughts,
my physical appearance.
At least my nose
worked a damn sight better
than your own.
You never knew
maternal love, paternal love –
only hatred and cruelty
in your frozen childhood.
Making love
to you was desperate,
an all-consuming need
to fill an empty, lonely space –
of course
it did not.

Washing Day

Elbow Lake, BC

Doing the weekly washing
        was a joy, a special day.
After all the men had gone
        to harvest cedar from the forest,
I'd gather up the clothes
        sort them in sunshine,
then I'd take buckets down
        to the lake, pausing,
so as not to scare the squirrel
        stretched out on a log –
but he'd wake, scamper up a tree
        to chatter at me angrily
from a high fir branch.

I'd gently step on wooden slats
        creating mirror ripples.
Maybe I'll see a moose today
        browsing in the shallows?
I never did, but occasionally
        a lonely loon called,
echoing from indigo mountains
        rippling back to me.
I'd run buckets back and forth,
        each time dipping carefully
from the wharf's deep end,
        peering down to see
land-locked Kokanee.*

While the clothes were drying
        I'd lie in dappled shade
planning evening menus
        for the cedar-cutting men.

* Kokanee: landlocked lake populations of sockeye salmon.

Wood Grain

Williams Lake, BC

Many hours I've spent
staring at timber-panelled walls
floors or ceilings,
tracing wood grain patterns,
contour lines,
smooth flowing,
tiny faces peering,
amber, mellow,
dark branch ears and eyes,
foxes, possums, hopping mice –
that daring little marten*
that once stole a chicken leg
when I left them thawing on the car –
one only for each hungry logger
eighty miles to town –
I went without myself.
This marten haunts me still.
I see him watching in my wooden floors
as he did that day
from high among spruce branches,
huge brown eyes and sharp teeth
gripping fiercely his prize
motionless, wooden
proud as sable.

*Marten: a weasel-like animal, trapped for the fur sable.

Chilcotin Fall

BC, 1980

Golden nectarine leaves make the sky bluer
they remind me of Chilcotin skies;
thought I'd never see a blue more vivid
against cottonwood's brilliant yellow,
each deepening the other's intensity.
Days were high plateau sunshine
nights froze quickly, quietly.
Snug in tent and sleeping bag
a huddled rush when we arose
to get a fire going
        and thaw the coffee pot.

From the Fraser to the sea
or at least to coastal mountains,
a million rolling grassland acres
deeply etched by icy rivers:
Chilko, Puntzi and Chilanko
join to pass through Farwell Canyon.
Dark Douglas fir and lodgepole pine
scarlet, crimson undergrowth
contrasting bare buff grass.
Sunlight glittering, reflecting off
Tatla, Taseko, Tatlayoko lakes.
The chroma of that autumn
was Chilcotin's best.
It seemed especially for me,
as if someone knew it was to be
        my last fall there.

Testing

Williams Lake, BC.

I felt your hands
go firm around my neck.
Fear welled,
an electric current surge
of self-preservation
instinctively said, 'Don't flinch.'
I raised my eyes to meet yours
full of bold friendship
and equality – no more –
that might have been too much.
I knew that you were close
to the edge. So was I,
but I had found a toehold
in the cliff face
where you had me dangling
for so long.
I found new bravery within –
can't recall what I said
but your fingers slowly loosened,
slipped away.
Later you confessed
how proud you were
of your self-control.
I breathe deeply –
even now,
remembering.

Mink

Botanic Beach, Vancouver Island, BC

A war baby,
>only girl
>>among the boys,

I inherited
>Father's independence,
>>Mother's insecurity.

This kept me
>on the fringe
>>of social groups.

Too old,
>too young
>>not quite belonging.

I've been alone
>most of my life.

I've enjoyed it,
>savoured it,
>>relished it,

even sought it
>on occasions.

Yet alone
>and lonely too
>>at times…

I would like to share
>a sunset's beauty,
>>a panoramic view,
>>>or secret glimpse

of nature's private life,
       like the Mink
              catching a breakfast fish
on an early morning beach.

Loon

Cariboo Region, BC

Across winter's lonely lake
the eerie call of a loon
echoes
through miles and long seasons,
shattering
here and now.

A Restless Wind

Basilica

Jardine St, Mt Gambier

Basilica bells and a rusty gate
commune with the restless wind,
sometimes sighing, sometimes crying,
sometimes singing in harmony.

Notes of sweetness after the heat
calling for rain from gathering clouds.
It fell to the north, so they're calling in vain
for north winds here are hot, and sere.

Fiftieth Summer

Still, grey air hung limply
>between over there and here,
almost damp, not yet cold
>it hid the sun all day,
leaving my world in limbo.
>It could be anytime,
anywhere, any season –
>like me,
between old-age and youth.

Too mature to take chances
>where youth hesitates not at all,
too old to have children who'd
>keep me up with modern trends,
too young to get a pension
>and forget financial woes,
too old to see humour
>in carefree happiness,
too young to cease caring
>about tomorrow
and old enough to lose my dreams.

Thin, moist air suspended –
>only scarlet gum blossom
speaks of country or of season.
>Where does that leave me
>>in my fiftieth summer?

Lime Marmalade

A tangy taste –
of sweet and sour all at once

conjuring images of sunny Spain,
English breakfast – boiled eggs and muffin.

Limes grow in the tropics, especially
to take heat from Tandoori.

Lemon, lime and Angostura bitters
quenches a monsoonal thirst.

A jar of liquid gold
with sunlight glowing through

sends me travelling the world
before the day's begun.

Is there time for one more slice of toast
before I leave for work?

Bill

I cut my lawn with a sickle once
my anger severed the grasses.
'Twas not my skill, or sweep,
nor the sharpness of the blade.

Lawnmower could not start
or would not start.
So I cursed the man who gave it.
'Good little machine,' he'd said.

But this was a superficial ire,
my anger was deep as coal.
I cursed the man I left behind
for he had asked me to go.
'Twas he who crushed my soul
then sent me on my way.

Then there were men who waited and watched
a single woman's faltering steps –
friends of friends,
sometimes even closer.
They'd swoop with words or deeds of kind
just long enough to build trust –
'You must be lonely…'
sexual favours soon expected.

It was the morning after an overture
from the husband of a close friend
that I cut my lawn with a sickle
when anger severed the grasses
not the sharpness of the blade.

Lawn Bowls

Subdued coloured cars roll up
precisely, on time
white ladies bubbling, pouring out
ebbing at car boots
to collect bowls bags
doors slamming.

Down the grade they flow
in rivulets like spilling milk
neat in hats
and hems of equal length
merging in confluence
through the clubhouse
and spread to soak life into
the square green delta.

Discipline

Old bowling ladies, regimented,
grew up through wars and discipline
continue now with uniforms just so.
Have their lives been governed
by husband, children, house?
Is this their escape?
Old? Are they?
More than I? Perhaps not?

I could never see myself
as they, having
adhered to timetables
rules, restrictions,
uniformity.

My pleasure would be
to wander,
to lose myself in scraggly scrub
wearing old clothes
among coloured birds and
wild, wild flowers.

Hey Diddle Diddle

It's easy to be cynical
when you are not the one in love –
she talks non-stop of what he does,
of what he says and plans.

Higher than the nursery cow
she thinks she has found 'the one'.
She's worshiping his every step
and he's stepped everywhere.

She assumes his knowledge is complete,
he fills her void with his words.
but those who come from other fields
see gaping discrepancies.

Is he the Fiddler or the Dish?
Is she the Dog or the Moon?
When he returns to his world and wife
will he take away her Spoon?

Morning Death

Jardine St, Mt Gambier

Light grey clouds
>	swept high by winds,
a warmer northerly,
>	neither hot nor cold.
The air swirls, eddies,
>	then stands motionless,
teasing dense foliage.

A sudden gust,
>	rattles the door,
moans through cracks,
>	a keening sigh,
bringing visions
>	of a windswept plain,
Blowaway grass piled
>	against invisible fences,
making hedges, high as me.

The wind then,
>	spoke not of death,
but of some unknown
>	secret sorrow – far away.

Now it speaks
>	of pain and death
while I,
>	in health and in sadness,
walk inside and wonder
>	what to have for breakfast.

Achievements

After all those years we spent together,
only recently have I been able
to remember any joy or good times –
they were mostly at the beginning.

My greatest achievement was
living through it cheerfully,
then going on to become another person.
I could not be as I was before.

She got lost somewhere –
a bitter but stronger woman emerged
who'd lost the gift of laughter.
I wonder what you gained?
I know your greatest achievement
was not killing me.
        You told me that.

From Mariachi to Jazz

Mexican

I never saw a Mexican
asleep beneath sombrero
beside saguaro cactus
in arid cowboy land.

I saw a place of steamy coasts
crumpled mountain ranges,
of high plateau – eternal spring
ravines steep and deep.

I saw ruins of ancient stone
where once blood was spilled
and the domes of Cortes' churches
atop archaic temples.

I saw a people groomed and proud
exploring their own realm,
dancing Indian patterns
in swirling cotton colours.

I saw the life of each town
flowing through their *zócalo*;
markets rich in food and colour
exposing the country's soul.

Teotihuacán

Mexico, 1990

I
had read
of Teotihuacán
ancient pyramids of
sun and moon, astronomical
accuracy beyond comprehension
never thinking I would see... Yet there
amid foundation ruins, before the tourists
and the heat, stretched The Street of the Dead
to Pyramid de Luna.   The Pyramid of the Sun was
east and huge –   two hundred steps and fifty –

Tlaloc
the   rain
god jutted from
Quetzalcoatl's Temple,
sunshine intensifying shadows.
Luna Plaza's sombrero seller wove
arms along his shoulder pole festooned by
hats. Butterfly palace, pink pillars carved with
Quetzal birds. It could have been a dream, but from
a broken wall I heard a piper's lilting notes, haunting the
early morning. And I'm sure the feathered serpent followed

us.

Olmec Heads*

Massive stone heads
emerge from the steamy swamps
of Tabasco.
Quarried one thousand years BC,
pitted now, or were you then?
Blank eyes stare blandly
from beneath headbands;
chins almost resting on the ground.
What secrets have you
locked inside your basalt brains?

Huge round boulders, giant marbles
gathered together
in Villahermosa park.
Among trees
and leafy dappled shade,
coatimundis† roam around,
silent paws, striped brush tails
waving, curling; following stealthily
mingling with undergrowth.
A curious combination…
were you watching
their great, great ancestors
on this swampy plateau?

* The Olmec were an ancient pre-Columbian civilisation living
in the tropical lowlands of Mexico, renowned for their artwork,
particularly the aptly named colossal heads, sculptured monoliths up
to three metres in height and several tons in weight.

† coatimundis: a type of raccoon

Mexico

Distant and mysterious Mexico,
Cortes conquered
left the Spanish imprint
deeper here than in Spain.
A morbid, bloody history
portrayed in black and red.
Deep shaded arches
face the square.
Domed cathedrals tower,
beside each village *zócalo*
to chime religion's hour.

Shop windows flaunt
bridal dresses to the poor,
wedding cakes of seven tiers,
high fashion leather shoes.
Iron grilles bar windows
in walls that shield
inner courtyards
sunlit green and friendly,
hidden from the hungry world.

Hammock

Mexico, 1990

I wish I could have given
this hammock to my mother
half a century ago.
Hot days sapped her strength.
Under casuarinas' shade
she would lie in an old cane chair.
It should have been a hammock.
She looked flushed and tired,
flat, I think she called it.
Tasselled casuarinas sighed
and whispered, creating
their own gentle breeze
to soothe her
until we came home from school.

Zócalo

Mexico, 1990

The *zócalo* is a living thing
in the heart of every town,
sometimes square,
sometimes not,
paved or paths with gardens.
Cathedral standing on one side,
stone arches on another
shade a dozen café tables.

Some have a rotunda
for mariachi bands,
seats for mothers' weary rest,
or for evening lovers later.
Children running, playing,
shining shoes for business men.
A small Indian girl
trying to sell
cloth dolls and coin purses.

The *zócalo* a gathering place,
a languorous place –
on fiesta days
a stage fills with vivid dancers.
Tourists sit, old men talk
people come and go
to feel the pulse of town.

Shaded seats are taken first
when noon heat pours down --
a place of cool greenery
soothing aching limbs
of those who've carried loads
from the hills to market;
a rest before trudging
home at end of day.

New Orleans

When I drove down to Louisiana
I saw pink azalea blooms.
The rain was grey,
        live oaks green,
dripping Spanish moss.

Back and forth wipers sloshed
to reveal a road awash
        miles of empty cane fields
a bleak and whitish swamp.

Grey, green and wet,
        wet, grey and green
misty pink glowed through,
a warm, sweet pink,
        like fairy floss,
spun sugar from the fields.

Mississippi, wild, muddy, brown
in an irritated mood
        lapped incessantly,
as we boarded a tourist launch.

Deckchairs slid toward the rails –
we feared for our lives.
        Square donuts and French coffee
revived us at the wharves.

Mansions antebellum white
beyond a mist of green,
        blurred by steady, sloping rain
as pink jazz cheered our souls.

Breast Cancer

1995

I made an appointment with my local GP and for some reason they fitted me in especially. When I got there I apologised, as I only needed a prescription which I could have ordered by phone. 'Well,' she said, 'while you're here, we'll do the full service!' She found two lumps in my left breast – 'Nothing to worry about, I think, but we'll check them anyway.'

At the mammogram they took about ten X-rays. My GP phoned me that evening to say that they had found an aggressive little lesion with tentacles right back against my chest wall. The other two were of no consequence – and in fact are still there!

Within a month I was back at work, a little lighter on the left and with a hollow armpit. Chance? Coincidence? Had it not been found then, I might not be here today.

Throughout my career I had encountered many patients with breast cancer, but never thought I would have to face the situation myself.

Premonition

Winter came early this year,
following summer,
with no announcement and no colour
as though a premonition.

Locals had mostly grizzled
about summer's heat.
There were days of glorious sunshine –
farmers called it dry.
Furtively, I stole moments
to frolic in the surf.

Soon the thermometer fell to icy nights,
fires and inside tasks returned.
Shrivelled leaves clung to trees –
even figs didn't ripen.
My body pointed me at death,
then slowly walked away.

Destiny

Mind blank

                        indigo sky

    hesitating

all the things which filled my life

        are distant

        dark sponge clouds, like my brain

too full to absorb   any more

    yet ready to release

                         moisture

drops of hope

    – or pain

as stoic tree trunks

                         question the wind

    my body

            in limbo

waiting

    poised

    for the incising blow

that will show

            my destiny.

Breast Cancer

1963: I see a chest devoid of breast
        all burnt and ulcerated,
  we moved to make more comfortable
        deep agony of lesion.
Sister working with me had been to Lae;
        we discussed the climate of New Guinea.

1983: I see a scar from umbilicus
        to halfway down an arm
each vessel tied off one by one
        nowadays diathermy.*
I helped close a wound as such
        with mattress stitches neat.

1995: I sense the tessellated spot
        moving near my ribs
tendrils penetrating deep,
        I felt pain last week before I knew.
Has it just begun? Or is it
        devouring my insides?

Is my body, which has spawned no child,
        so desperate that it needs
to grow an alien 'thing'
        within my breast?
And like a child would have,
        this 'thing' will change my life.

---

* Diathermy is an instrument which seals blood vessels using an electrical current eliminating the time-consuming need for individual tying.

May '95, Thinking…

Rivoli Bay, SA

It was something in the angle of the sun –
an ethereal light,
glowing from soft young foliage,
reflecting on marine blue,
unreal, as though part of me
had already gone.
If I die, will Barbara and Carol be there too?
Or maybe Bernard Henry?

I will never climb to Machu Picchu
nor feel the chill Canadian fall
with yellow, brilliant yellow:
never again be hugged
by warm sweet tropic climes;
nor take a train
across the Russian steppes;
never bathe in azure waves and
stinging salty foam.

Sky is streaked with windswept clouds
thin and high.

How much difference have I made?
None in truth.
And who will write to tell
my friends in foreign places
after I have gone?

Fog

Jardine St, Mt Gambier

A fog came down this morning,
        unexpectedly,
after the sun had
        shone for a while
I'd already started the washing.
        It was my first
day off for the week,
        and this giant sponge
soaked up all my enthusiasm
        rinsed away happiness and
suspended everything
        limply in the yard.
An apple thudded
        to the ground.

Nasturtiums

Jardine St, Mt Gambier

Nasturtiums clambering
>   on an old wooden fence
in a riot of
>   orange and green,
evoke glimpses
>   of an era past:
bright pink geraniums,
>   plum-red hollyhocks
and delphiniums blue
>   as willow pattern.
Cups of tea,
>   cucumber sandwiches
and the steady hum of bees.

Green Tea and Rice

Siam Morning

Hear the wind chimes?
Bamboo calling
on a tropic breeze.
Dew-fresh flowers
for the House God
shrine upon gatepost.
Keep us free from evil spirits.
Gecko clicking from the ceiling
flicking tongue to clear his sight.

Curd and Treakle

Sri Lanka

Serendib: a teardrop isle in Indian seas
    warm waves lapping palm-shaded toes.
        Tigers, deer in thorny scrub.
Ancient cities – Anura dha pura.
    Poson's* pilgrims in Polonnaruwa,
        camped on Bund levee.
Frescoes on Sigiriya Rock
    six hundred feet above;
        chalk-white dagoba domes
            to pray for Buddha's peace.
Watch-house for elephants
    steps to tree look-out.
        Curfew in Trincomalee
            a hint of stormy weather.
Colourful Tamil saris dot
        green, tea groomed hillsides.
Masked torch bearers, dancers drumming
        in Kandy's bejewelled parade.
Chill mountains
    lemon grass growing wild.
Curd and treacle –
    jaggery sugar from the palm
        sweet poverty and beauty
    curdled in blood and death.

* Poson: a festival for the June full moon

Mangoes 1

Through an ice-white winter
in a Canadian grocery store
I paused to smell sweet mangoes.

So expensive, I could not justify…
but closed my eyes and dreamt
of thick, sweet, humid air,
indolent tropic days,
the sensuous pleasure of fluids
to be imbibed or bathed in
and fruit, sweet fruit to devour.

I grew up in cool damp climes
far from where the mango grows,
so why should they
speak to me of freedom?

Mangoes 2

Each morning on the Maldives,
I slurped golden fruit
from a huge and shady mango tree
in the yard – white coral-walled.
Houseboys would pick one daily,
then leave it, fresh
and glowing on the table.

In the heat of Ramadan
watching white dusty streets
with long waiting water queues
I sat cool, sipping tea
and eating mango
sweet, juicy, minty mango
in the shade.

Nirvana

My material needs are not great –
I enjoy small pleasures.
Already it is too late to share many things
other couples take for granted.
I should have chosen differently,
but there was little left by the time
I got to the table. I just accepted
what was offered, gratefully at first,
threw one back, left one there,
what shall I do with the third?

Remnants were either half eaten or mouldy.
I looked within myself until I was inside-out.
I walked through a band of flame,
failed the elephant* in theory,
faced lion, horse and bull.
I searched lush vines for vitality –
maybe I should follow the goose
to find the lotus of Nirvana, so that I need
nothing and no one, ever.

---

* The elephant is the symbol for birth – I had failed my midwifery exams.

Mandalay Music

Burma, 1986

Am I awake? Am I dreaming?
It's all so unreal.
What is that whirring,
so pervading…
not continuous, yet continuing,
a background chorus?
Frogs!

I open my eyes,
Stars blur in warm darkness.
I remember now; I've been ill…
we need to be at the wharf,
the Irrawaddy ferry leaves at five.
Bicycle wheels on wet roadway
whirr, whirr; whirr, whirr.
A sleeping dog
rises slowly from
warm road
out of our path.

I close my eyes and drift;
cello croaks of bullfrogs
reverberate intermittently
through the purple morning.

Kites

Port MacDonnell, SA

Delta kite an angry hornet in brisk autumn breeze
bucking and straining against its string
eager to lose itself among brooding clouds.

We had a box kite* when I was a child,
bright yellow from the war,
neat wires to fold, pack away until another day.

Other children glued sticks and string,
diamond kites from 'How to' book instructions
to fly and tangle in telephone wires.

Graceful freedom symbols tentatively tied to the ground,
a choreography of the wind,
whirling green and orange tubes, red fish or yellow sleds.

I've seen pictures of Japan: one hundred strings connecting
fluttering colours to a crowd;
dragon kites from China – ten metres long at least;

huge moon kites from Kota Baru, all brocade and tassels;
hexagonal *rokkaku* from Japan,
stacks and stripes and parafoils, billowing, pulsating.

And our pink, blue and purple delta stalled,
whispered to the wind, then
hissed a hundred figure eights against a stormy sky.

---

* The box kite was invented by the Australian Lawrence Hargrave in 1893. Military uses involved a kite/radio transmitter combination issued to pilots during World War II for use in life rafts.

Malaysian Pewter

Indigo mountains fading
to violet
then dusty blue,
mirrored in the shallow dams
calm and still as glass.
Ducks pairing off
silhouetted shapes flapping.
Dull pewter sky –
with lighter patches and
steely strips,
like the mug Jim bought from Selangor
– twice the price
we'd seen elsewhere;
and burnished as
Malaysian skies that day.

Charcoal and Ashes

Fire

I was always afraid of fire as a child, when wood stove and open hearth were our only source of cooking and heating. We were taught to have respect and to be very careful with campfires or incinerators. I have also seen the heart-breaking damage and injury that bushfires cause to vegetation, property and animals, wild and domestic.

In 2000, after a lifelong curiosity about the mysterious southern continent of the Americas, a sort of 'P' tacked precariously onto its northern neighbour – trailing by the thread of Panama, I took two months' annual leave, three months' long service leave and some leave without pay to explore this continent of contrasts.

While visiting the swampy Pantanal region of Brazil, I got the news that my little cottage in Mount Gambier had burnt down in the middle of the night, four days earlier. At that time I had been impatiently waiting for a train in central Bolivia – I was on edge, worried about news from home. My mother was quite elderly – but it wasn't her that caused this feeling of unease. It was, according to the thirteen emails, my house. I was stunned with disbelief.

No one knows the cause, probably electrical, perhaps a mouse chewed through a wire. How quickly life's mementos disappeared or were damaged.

With Apologies to Friedrich Nietzsche

When my house burned down
                I could not eat my dinner,
    but out of its ashes will
                hopefully come my next meal…

To 19 Jardine Street

Postwar born and built –
                with only available materials
four wooden rooms –
                outside bathroom, loo and laundry.
Your builder planted
                careful trees designed to shield
from winter winds
                and feed with many fruits,
a succession
                of owners who added and divided.

I found you,
                neglected, overrun
by dogs and
                weeds one metre high.
Peeled by degree,
                your soul emerged
to welcome my
                guests from foreign lands.

Painted, patched, embellished
                we nurtured each other.
Despite chooks
                or possibly because of,
our garden
                smiled on all seasons.
Street drivers
                hardly noticed steep
cottage roof
                beyond multicoloured leaves.

Again,
                distant travel called me.
I did not
                witness your pain –
your lonely
                violent death.

Now, street drivers
                hardly notice your
blackened eyes,
                your charred body
flowerless spring garden,
                black-edged in silence
but muted by
                green's healing tones.

Adrift

    Stories trail…

        with no endings
            pictures awaiting frames…

                wait no more.
                Countless dreams,
          now thin as smoke
       drift …

    history crackling…

melts to oblivion.
    Half-written verse…

        floats ash-grey
            stored sketches, notes,
      colours curdled
           fragments falter,
                future fails,
                    holding its breath.

Threads

Hollow house filled with debris
rotting, broken, charred.
My fragile life, barely gathered,
hardly sorted – to chronology.

Eerie wind whistling through wall gaps
stirs black remnants –
tattered fragments of memory,
threadbare now.

I had plans or dreams
to weave or knit this assortment
into decorative garments
or artistic works.

Hold, tenuous at best,
blackened threads slip altogether
from my fingers.

Roof creaks, teeters – a lid barely on.
Crooked refrigerator door
opens, closes,
a dull tapping, flapping.

An empty breeze flutters shreds
out along the street
and into gutters…

Paper Phantoms

Grey wind swirling scraps of paper,
        circular with blackened edges,
flipping, wheeling over bare ground,
        gathering with other pages trapped among
dying shrubs along the fence line.
        Fluttering perimeter decorations,
as in vast rubbish tips or
        where Columbia meets Venezuela.

One falters near my feet,
        familiar writing – I stoop and stare,
words penned by my father,
        gone these two years now,
a segment, out of sequence,
        thoughts live on past lifespan,
subject obscured by a smudge.

A sudden gust lifts it, rolls
        a rounded book, careering to join
three half *National Geographic* pages,
        worldly pictures fading;
several printed poetry sheets, curling;
        others blurred or crinkled
by water blasts, sent to save,
        but, successfully drowning
                all remnants of my past.

Homesick

For one who travelled to odd corners
        just to see how others lived,
        to feel their weather,
        taste their food,
it's strange.

For one who shopped in coloured markets,
        buying strange exotic fruits;
        boiled coffee over campfires,
        or through a light globe socket,*
it's strange.

For one who slept on bunks or floors,
        or hammocks under stars,
        who awoke to greet dawn
        in new exciting lands,
it's strange.

For one who tramped steep, narrow streets,
        alpine meadows, coastal sands
        even steamy jungle trails,
        this malaise
is strange.

I want to wander in my garden
        among my trees.
        I need my home,
        my Nan's deckchair
                my pantry, my books, my bed.
It's strange.

---

* We had an electric immerser to boil water, and if there were no power points, took out light globe and held immerser in contact until water boiled – 110 volts not 240!

Numb

Numb for weeks,
sudden fingers of reality
touch my skin
bringing wakeful nights.

Under cover of darkness
forgotten hurts or
perspiring panic
emerge to scream
'Fire'!

Rebuilding –
slow logic
in apparent stoic calm.

Forty

'I don't want to be forty, and have nothing,' she said to me.
I was and had nothing.
She was not: had a home, a farm, two children.
I didn't know she was planning escape,
leaving everything including husband –
taking only her children,
to start again with someone else.

Twenty years later, she has two more children,
a full, busy life,
with accolades from all the town.
While I, again at crossroads,
have nothing. My home and life a shell.
Words of friends flicker around edges
licking at my numbness.

Changing Weather

Magpies

Today I heard a magpie call.
It's a sound that I know well.
As a child, their carolling
woke me every morning.
On warm summer afternoons
in the quiet shade of trees
the magpie sits and talks –
a soft warbling reverie,
each refrain ending
with careful mimicry –
a neigh, a bark, another bird –
I've even heard them chopping wood
complete with echoing axe-fall.

In years abroad, I missed their cheery note
until I heard, in white and navy winter
atop a tall, straight cedar pole –
a glossy raven –
with deeper throaty warble.
Not the breadth of repertoire
but similar enough –
to make me homesick.

I love the magpies'
haunting, lilting call,
occasionally a strident note
to emphasise a point.

Red Flags

Jardine St, Mt Gambier

There is a cold, dry northerly blowing,
        unusual for here
                in this damp, southern clime.
A winter desert wind
        with cool sun brightly shining.
                I must have felt this wind before
blowing down from Broken Hill
        across the anabranch,
                complete with red dust tinge.
But no, I feel it's from the Steppes.
        Suddenly I see Beijing,
                shivering in my coat.
A dry, metal wind bringing
        tastes of Mongolia.
                I remember excitement,
foreignness, and
        familiarity too.
I shiver again in cold, dry wind
        which flutters the last
                tattered red flags
                        from my apple tree.
An invisible stream
        of hopeful people
                march towards change.
I hang my washing slowly
        in this arid northerly…

Confetti

My plum tree's thousand sticks
are showered with confetti
from the wedding of
wind and rain and sun.

Seasons

Thoughts from Mt Gambier, SA

Though many poets write of spring,
>   it's never thrilled me much.
I love summer mornings
>   fresh with clear skies.
Fleet screech screech of lorikeet
>   from scarlet blossoms tree to tree.

I love summer evenings,
>   preferably by water
turquoise sea or river deep
>   to bathe away the day,
silken air and starlight,
>   cicadas singing praises.

I love autumns everywhere
>   with days of liquid gold,
cool, damp, misty mornings
>   and fruit, fresh fruit to pick,
marbled magpie voices
>   plovers' staccato cries.

The tropics have no springtime
>   there's only Wet or Dry.

When I lived in northern climes
>   I almost hated spring,
dragging winter miserably on,
>   icy, dangerous roads
the year's collected garbage
>   revealed by melting snow.

Budding of the willows meant
        a long, long time till summer yet.

Sometimes Mount Gambier's winter rain
        drips on to Christmas time.
Cootamundra briefly
        yellows our July,
spring sneaks subtly in from there.

This year the sun has smiled
        streets blossomed pink and madder,
bulbs brilliantly burst in every hue,
        golden wattle, yellow daisies,
a dozen shades of mauve or blue,
        pollen on the puddles.

Next week the wind will be
        plum petal laden,
whirling, dancing, celebrating.

Balancing Lovers

One is loving mostly
but never making love,
another's tongue is bitter,
daily love a desperate need.

Was there a Latin lover
who only came at night
with *brioso* music
to stir my very soul?

I knew a sailor once
but he was never home.
A carpenter with mind
like warped wood.
Later, I heard, he beat
his pregnant wife.

If there was a melting pot
to stir and blend them all,
would a compromise emerge?
Are scales* meant to measure,
balance or protect?

---

* Scales:
1. thin, hard, flat plates that form covering of a surface – e.g. fish
2. a progression of steps
3. a balancing device
4. a graduated line for measuring proportion

Monsoon

Summer rain, fat and heavy;
    I love it.
Yet it brings depression
    and a kind of loneliness.
Raining all across the nation
    squelching
allowing fire fighters
    to rest.
Raining now in Darwin
    renewing life in Kakadu
waterbirds will flock and feast,
    would that I could be there too.
The leaking roof we thought was fixed
    drips steadily into
strategic flowerpot.

Rain is cutting roads throughout
    The Centre
stranding tourists,
    in red, red mud.

Warm, sweet, cloying rain
    quenching
thirsty garden beds,
    soaking
body and mind with memories
    of rain in other places,
laughing with damp people,
    who I will never see again.

Toothmarks

The bite of summer's heat
>has loosened on this day.
The breeze, once
>searing northerly
has eased to western skies,
>leaving only tooth marks
in the blue.

Amber

Jardine St, Mt Gambier

An amber light has filled the sky,
cast its glow on my home.

So involved was I in savouring
this glorious summer day,
that it ended before I realised.

Crescendo of cicada chorus,
there's just a hint of smoke –
no wind, not a flicker of breeze.

Warmth and light fade gradually –
as cooling embers.
A honeyeater family
fills the air with acrobatics
and haunting, piping calls.

A single star, a sickle moon –
there is peace in this
garden full of weeds.

www.ingramcontent.com/pod-product-compliance
Lightning Source LLC
Chambersburg PA
CBHW070915080526
44589CB00013B/1300